The Buddha's Guide to Men's Style

Fashion with Compassion

Table of Contents

Chapter 1. Introduction

Welcome to a remarkably illuminating voyage through the world of men's fashion, seen through a transfixing Buddhist lens. "The Buddha's Guide to Men's Style: Fashion with Compassion" offers you an exciting new perspective on sartorial elegance, blending contemporary men's style with ancient Buddhist wisdom in a way you've probably never imagined. This special report promises to not only inspire your wardrobe but also unwrap the profound threads of mindfulness and empathy meticulous stitched into your everyday fashion choices. Embark on this enlightening exploration with us and breath fresh life into your style, promoting both internal tranquility and visible sophistication. Step into the world where clothing does more than just speaking about your personality; it echoes the compassionate, wise, humble man within you. So, if you're ready to infuse a fresh energy into your style, to embody compassion through your attire, and stand out from the crowd effortlessly, this special report is a must-have!

Chapter 2. An Introduction to Buddha's Principles and Men's Fashion

Our journey begins at the confluence of two seemingly disparate worlds - that of Buddhism, a path to spiritual enlightenment, and men's contemporary fashion, a world of aesthetics, standing and self-expression. While on the surface, these fields may appear disconnected, a deeper dive reveals numerous parallels and possibilities for alignment. By weaving these threads together, we unfold an enriching tapestry that lends greater depth to our daily sartorial choices by imbuing our attire with elements of mindfulness, enlightenment, compassion, and humility borne of Buddhist teachings.

2.1. Buddhism: A Primer for Enlightenment

Embarking upon this exploration, we must first familiarize ourselves with basic Buddhist principles. Born in the northeastern Indian subcontinent, Buddhism emanated from the teachings of Siddhartha Gautama, widely known as Buddha. Buddha journeyed through life seeking answers to free mankind from suffering – his journey and teachings are encapsulated in the Four Noble Truths and the Noble Eightfold Path.

The Four Noble Truths are:

1. The Truth of Suffering: Life is fraught with turmoil, including disease, old age, and death.

2. The Truth of the Cause of Suffering: Desire and ignorance are at the root of suffering.

3. The Truth of the End of Suffering: Eliminating desire and ignorance brings an end to suffering.

4. The Truth of the Path: The path to the cessation of suffering is the Noble Eightfold Path.

This Path seeks to cultivate right understanding, thinking, speech, action, livelihood, effort, mindfulness, and concentration to guide individuals away from ignorance and towards enlightenment, peace, and freedom from suffering. It encourages the cultivation of wisdom, ethical conduct, and mental development.

2.2. Clothing: A Canvas of Self-Expression

Next, we shift focus towards clothing – an indispensable element of modern human life. Clothes do far more than provide protection against environmental elements. They serve as a reflection of personal identity, societal status, and ambition. They are, in essence, an expression of self.

In more recent times, the men's fashion industry has seen a revolution. Meaning and depth are fervently sought in every sartorial decision. Styles have risen that embody moods, eras, movements, and even philosophies. Amidst this, striding the path of enlightenment with sartorial flair seems like a natural progression.

2.3. Harmonizing Principles of Buddhism with Men's Fashion

Straddling two worlds, one of enlightenment and compassion, the other of aesthetics and individualism, might seem like a balancing act. But acknowledging the depth and breadth of each domain, we can find synergies that enable us to express our evolving spiritual self.

1. Mindful Dressing: Just as mindfulness underpins Buddhism, applying mindfulness to your sartorial decisions can enhance your connection with yourself and your environment, echoing Buddhist beliefs. Choosing natural materials acknowledges the beauty of the natural world, while selecting designs that fit well and give comfort reflects self-care and respect for your body.

2. Compassionate Choices: Embracing compassionate dressing encourages greater empathy. By opting for ethically and sustainably sourced garments, you exhibit a commitment to reducing harm, protecting labor rights, and promoting sustainability - indeed a trait of the enlightened.

3. Humility and Simplicity: Buddhism teaches us that desire breeds suffering. By embracing humility and simplicity in your style, one can circumvent the unfettered desire rife in the world of fashion, opting to express oneself subtly and genuinely, freed from the burden of materialistic pursuits.

2.4. Infusing Compassion into Your Style

As we navigate the world of fashion, consuming and discarding, we run the risk of perpetuating cycles of harm, greed, and desire. The heedless pursuit of trends can fuel an industry fraught with unethical labor practices, harm to our environment, and mindless consumption. By choosing to infuse compassion into our style, we can promote mindful consumption, encourage sustainability, and uphold ethical labor practices, all while curating a wardrobe that speaks to our values, our style, and our desire for a just world.

Whether it's selecting organic cotton shirts, fair-trade accessories, or cruelty-free footwear, each decision can be a mindful act of compassion, aligning us closer to Buddhist teachings. This learning extends beyond a well-rounded wardrobe; understanding that fashion can either draw us closer to enlightenment or perpetuate desire and suffering has lifelong implications for how we engage with the world around us.

Through this chapter, we have embarked on an enlightening exploration, demonstrating how Buddhist principles can marry everyday fashion decisions, adding a layer of depth, compassion, and mindfulness to men's style, transcending it from mere self-expression to conscious action. As our journey continues, we will delve deeper into the synergies between Buddhist principles and specific areas of men's fashion, offering practical examples and advice to inspire you on your path to fashion enlightenment.

Chapter 3. The Art of Mindful Dressing

Mindful dressing is not just about combining colors, patterns, and fabrics. It is the union of consciousness and attire, the embodiment of compassion and empathy in our style choices, and the realization of the interconnectedness of all things — from the thread of our clothes to the spiritual thread that ties us all. When we dress mindfully, we are not merely donning garments; we are draping ourselves in our values, our beliefs, and our character.

3.1. Mindful Dressing: A Conceptual Overview

The initial step towards mindful dressing involves understanding its essence. Unlike conventional dressing, which prioritizes external factors such as appearance and trends, mindful dressing gives precedence to inner values like awareness and intention. It is dressing with cognizance, weaving compassion into the fabric of your style, and integrating the Buddhist principle of mindfulness into the realm of men's fashion. This approach interlocks the philosophical wisdom with sartorial elegance, redefining the concept of men's style.

3.2. The Universal Thread: Connection with the World

One key cornerstone of Buddhist philosophy is the understanding of interconnectedness, the realization that everything is linked in some way. When we apply this concept to mindful dressing, it involves being conscious of the way our fashion choices affect those around us and the world at large. The garments you choose to wear are an extension of this connection. Being mindful in this sense includes recognizing the environmental impact of the production process, acknowledging the economic realities of the workers who made your garments, and promoting brands that prioritize fair-trade and sustainability.

3.3. Dressing with Intention: Beyond Fabrics and Colors

Dressing with intention is another integral aspect of mindful dressing. Each day we consciously decide what we will wear, whether for an important meeting, a casual outing, or a night out. But when you dress mindfully, you're not only selecting clothes based on their aesthetic appeal or the occasion. You're considering how those clothes make you feel, the values they represent, and their impact on your self-image. This intentionality injects a sense of purpose into your everyday style, connecting you with the garments on a deeper level.

3.4. Style as an Act of Self-Care

Mindful dressing is in part, an act of self-care. When we consciously choose our garments, we engage in self-expression, asserting our identity, and embracing our uniqueness. However, there's more to it than that. When we lovingly care for our clothes—washing them carefully, neatly arranging them in our wardrobes—we learn to appreciate them more, developing a stronger sense of gratitude. This, in turn, influences the amount of care we put into selecting our clothes, enhancing our overall approach to style.

3.5. Rethinking Trends: Embracing Timelessness

Part of mindful dressing is stepping away from the passing tides of fast fashion and turning towards the shores of timelessness. Constantly chasing trends can cultivate a mindset of insatiability, always wanting the next "in" thing. However, Buddhism teaches us the dangers of craving, leading to dukkha, or suffering. Instead, embrace the beauty of classic, enduring pieces. Slow fashion not only leads to a wardrobe filled with garments you truly love and value but also lessens the overall impact on the environment, promoting a more sustainable lifestyle.

3.6. Everyday Enlightenment: Wearing Your Values

When we practice enlightened dressing, we bring enlightenment into our everyday lives. This means seeing beyond the pure material value of the clothes we wear and recognizing the moral and spiritual values they embody. Whether it's a shirt produced by a brand that pays fair wages, a pair of shoes created using sustainable materials, or a tie that you inherited from your grandfather, each piece tells a story. When you dress mindfully, you weave these stories into your own, creating a wardrobe that is much more than a collection of clothes—it's an echo of your values, a manifestation of your conscious choices, a reflection of your inner self.

Mindful dressing intertwines the fibers of fashion and compassion, interweaving the threads of the external and internal world. It takes the practice of fashion beyond mere physicality and plants it firmly within the spiritual and moral realm. By consciously choosing what we wear and understanding the far-reaching effects of these decisions, we cultivate a deeper connection with ourselves and the world around us. In essence, mindful dressing transforms the act of clothing oneself into a meditation, a deliberate practice of self-awareness, compassion, and interconnectedness. By embracing this approach to style, you embrace the beauty of consciousness, care, and compassion—enhancing not just your wardrobe, but your character too.

Chapter 4. The Intersection of Simplicity and Sophistication

The Buddhist philosophies guide about the beauty of simplicity, propounding the concept of less being more. Paralleling this wisdom to the realm of men's fashion conjectures a vivid image of sophistication achieved not through extravagance, but through a few calculated, mindful choices. Albeit intimidating, this perceived contradiction might hold the secret to crafting your quintessential modern man's wardrobe.

4.1. The Essence of Simplicity

Reflecting on our Buddhist teachings, we learn that the practice of simplicity or "minimalism" is intricately linked to the concept of "less is more." This ethos is not restricted to the realm of material possessions but is also indicative of one's personal style. The elegance of simplicity should not be mistaken as synonymous to monotony. On the contrary, it brings forth the philosophy of appreciating the core essence of each garment, accessory, and ensemble, sans the distractions of over-accessorization or ostentatious displays of wealth.

The primary purpose of this form of dressing is to promote comfort, functionality, and the thoughtful use of clothes to express one's true self, without leaning towards extravagance. This elegantly composed symphony of clothes does not scream for attention; rather, it subtly captures the attention in its serene disposition.

4.2. The Understated Art of Sophistication

Sophistication, in the context of men's fashion, is not merely an expression of fabric filigree, textured patterns, and intricately designed accessories. Rather, it's an art form, reflecting a complete personality. Sophistication is inherent rather than acquired, subtly asserted rather than blatantly expressed. It defines how a certain outfit is curated and worn with grace and subtlety, making a statement without the need for verbosity.

Embracing sophistication allows you to immerse in the essence of the garment, respecting its true value it possesses beyond the apparent materialism. That is where simplicity and sophistication become allies in men's fashion, challenging the very norms and conjecturing an extraordinary style etiquette.

4.3. Simplicity and Sophistication Interlude: The Modern Man's Wardrobe

Taking cues from the minimalist approach, your clothing choices should be based on intention and purpose, rather than following trends blindly. This subtle shift in approach can create ensembles that are truly timeless in their making. A lean, well-curated wardrobe comprises some foundational pieces that can be mixed and matched to create both casual and formal looks.

You could start with well-tailored suits in classic shades of black, navy, and charcoal grey, paired with crisp white or light blue dress shirts. These, combined with exquisite silk ties in muted tones, can create a versatile palette. A well-fitted blazer with tailored trousers or chinos complements by a Polo shirt or a turtleneck for a business-casual style or a relaxed yet refined weekend look. Couple these with essential accessories like a wristwatch with a classic dial, lace-up oxfords, or timeless loafers to complete the ensemble.

This modern wardrobe exemplifies the intersection of simplicity and sophistication, blending the lines between aesthetics and functionality.

4.4. Mindful Selection and Care

A conscious selection process is essential to building a wardrobe that resonates with the principles of simplicity and sophistication. Opt for quality over quantity, investing in a few high-quality pieces that last longer and have a lesser environmental footprint.

Remember, care is a crucial part of maintaining the life of your garments. Being mindful of your clothes' needs, such as particular cleaning instructions or storage conditions, ensures their longevity. This mindfulness towards your possessions eventually breeds into other aspects of life, promoting peace, contentment, and, ultimately, leading to the path of enlightenment.

4.5. The Echo of Your Inner Self

Styles can change, trends may come and go, but your unique perception of fashion woven with Buddhist philosophies can transcend the jaded norms and influence your style journey profoundly. Your attire serves as a reflection of your inner self, an echo of your experiences manifesting in your choice of clothing and the way you carry it.

With simplicity and sophistication as the fundamental pillars, this unique approach to men's fashion bridges the chasm between style and substance. You embark on a journey beyond the confines of traditional fashion, venturing into a realm where your clothes mirror your inner, compassionate, wise, humble self.

By blending simplicity and sophistication into your style statement, you not only invite admiration from others, but you also command respect for your mindfulness and thoughtful approach towards fashion. And this radiates the very essence of a stylish Buddhist man - uncomplicated, sophisticated, and connected bodhisattva, in the arena of life and style.

In closing, striking a balance between simplicity and sophistication is more than just an aesthetic venture. It is a mindful journey into exploring one's personal style - a journey where every piece of clothing is a stitch in the fabric of your consciousness and your assertive journey into mindfulness through sartorial choices.

Chapter 5. Creating Balance - The Middle Path in Fashion

Before embarking on any journey, it's imperative to understand the terrain, the landmarks, and the intended destination. In our voyage through the expansive world of men's fashion, the understanding of a foundational concept is critical — balance. The very essence of Buddhism hinges on this notion and locates its sanctity within the Middle Path, the practice of neither excessive self-indulgence nor self-denial. A principle as important as this finds its manifestation in several aspects of life, including the way we present ourselves — our style.

5.1. The Concept of Balance

Balance is the point of equilibrium where elements contributing to a system are in accordance. The fashion industry, laden with various designs, trends, and expressions, also gravitates towards this center of stability. Achieving balance in fashion implies curating a wardrobe that is not excessively driven by the whims of changing trends, nor is overly conservative or archaic. Instead, it is a harmonious blend of the modern and the traditional, the daring and the modest, the vibrant and the muted. Being stylish doesn't mean relinquishing comfort, or the other way round. Balance in fashion is about a practical amalgamation of personal comfort, lifestyle needs, and fashion sense.

In the context of Buddhism, this philosophy is the cornerstone of Buddha's teachings. Known as the Middle Path, it's about avoiding extremes and sustaining balance in all aspects of life, including relationships, possessions, and yes, personal style. The Middle Path in fashion, like in life, leads to a happier, healthier, and more content self.

5.2. Recognizing the Weight of Extremes

To understand balance, we need to recognize what it counteracts — extremes. While adorning ourselves with the trendiest fashion items might appease our fashion-conscious side, it could lead to an overemphasis on external aesthetics, conflicting with our comfort, practicality, and financial prudence. On the other hand, completely ceding to comfort over style could result in an unrefined or mundane appearance. The age of the reclusive monk fashion has passed.

Understanding these extremes and the consequences they carry is the first stride towards the Middle Path. Like Buddha taught his disciples, recognizing the state of imbalance can set the foundation for achieving balance. Visualize your prevalent style: do you find yourself heavily leaned towards one extreme or another? If so, it might be a sign to reformulate your sartorial choices.

5.3. The Elements of Fashion and Balance

Creating balance in fashion is not about compromising on your individual style or personality. It's about harmonizing the various elements of fashion. These elements could include colors, patterns, materials, and layers.

Colors - Try to strike a balance between attention-grabbing vibrant tones and calming, neutral hues. An excessive use of either could make your wardrobe seem redundant.

Patterns - Similar to colors, patterns should also contain a balanced mixture of flamboyant, bold designs and understated, classic ones.

Materials - A balanced wardrobe should house a variety of clothing materials, each fulfilling different functional requisites like temperature regulation, comfort, and aesthetics.

Layers - While multi-layered attire can add depth to your style, not every occasion calls for it. Strike a balance in your style by speckling single-layered outfits among your layered ensembles.

5.4. Guidelines to the Middle Path in Fashion

The Middle Path in fashion doesn't necessarily indicate a precise rule-book to follow. However, keeping certain guidelines in mind can assist in making mindful styling decisions.

Consider Function and Comfort - Fashion should not overshadow the primary function of clothes: protection and comfort. Alongside style, pay heed to the comfort and suitability of an attire considering the weather, occasion, and your personal comfort.

Mindful Consumption - The Middle Path admonishes against extreme consumption or utter renouncement. When shopping, be mindful of your requirements and the long-term utility of what you are buying.

Harmonious Coordination - Maintain a sense of harmony in your outfit by attuning your color palettes, patterns, accessories, and overall attire to each other.

Experimenting with Moderation - Lastly, while it is good to experiment with different styles and trends, do so in moderation. For every bold, standout piece you add to your wardrobe, include a timeless, subtle piece as well.

Building a balanced wardrobe is not an exercise you complete overnight. It's a process, requiring thoughtful reflection, mindful actions, and consistent efforts. So, take your time and remember, style is a way of communicating your personality. Let it reflect your best self!

Chapter 6. Dressing Consciously: Sustainable Fashion Choices

Starting off on the path towards incorporating sustainable habits into our daily wardrobe choices can feel daunting. But, remember the wise Buddha words – "Be where you are; otherwise, you will miss your life." When applied to fashion, it means starting from where you stand—right now—and making incremental changes towards more conscious choices.

6.1. Understanding Sustainable Fashion

We begin by addressing the elephant in the room – what is sustainable fashion? The term is often misunderstood and conflated with other fashion movements such as ethical fashion. In the simplest terms, sustainable fashion refers to clothing that respects the environment and the people involved in its production – stable work conditions, fair wages, and no harm to the environment. It calls for the use of eco-friendly materials, reduced water consumption, and minimized waste production. But, it's not merely about the processes; it's about the human act of wearing and treating clothes with respect and consciousness.

6.2. Relating to Your Clothes

Connecting with your clothing is the first step towards the conscious consumerism that defines sustainable fashion. Start with considering the clothes you already own. How often do you wear them? How do you care for them? Are you aware of the materials used in them?

Begin to see your clothes as more than just shapes and colors that adhere to the trends of the season. Understand what they represent, where they come from, and the impact they have on the world.

6.3. Addressing Fast Fashion Practices

One of the most significant impediments to sustainable fashion is the fast fashion industry. Fast fashion is characterized by inexpensive, trend-based clothing that gets produced rapidly by mass-market retailers. The issue here is that clothes are used and discarded at a swift rate, leading to pollution and waste.

The Buddhist principle of non-harm can be brought into play here. By making mindful fashion choices and rejecting the ephemeral nature of trends, we can reduce the demand for fast fashion. Opt for timeless styles that can be repeated again and again without sacrificing sartorial elegance, and don't fall prey to the lure of regular shopping.

6.4. Practicing Mindful Shopping

Mindful shopping is the heart of sustainable fashion. It involves buying less, choosing well, and making it last. When shopping for new clothes, consider these important aspects:

- Material: Opt for natural, eco-friendly materials like organic cotton, linen, or hemp that have a smaller ecological footprint. Shun synthetic fabrics like polyester, nylon, and spandex that take hundreds of years to decompose.

- Ethics: Research brands and only support those that treat workers fairly and prioritize sustainable practices.

- Longevity: Choose items of high quality that will withstand repeated wear and washing.

Remember, every purchase is a vote for the kind of world you want to live in.

6.5. Embracing Versatility & Minimalism

The Buddhist principle of simplicity directly translates to the wardrobe with the concept of a capsule wardrobe. The aim is to maintain a collection of versatile clothes that effectively meet your day-to-day needs, without the excess. This not only supports sustainable fashion by reducing the demand for clothing production but also helps maintain cleanliness and order in life, something greatly emphasized in Buddhist teachings.

6.6. Mending & Recycling

Closely related to sustainable fashion is the art of mending and recycling. It aligns directly with the Buddhist philosophy of impermanence, recognizing that nothing is broken – it merely transforms. So, when your clothes start to show signs of wear and tear, don't simply throw them away; instead, learn to mend them or repurpose them to serve another function.

6.7. Lifelong Learning and Adaptation

The journey towards sustainable fashion isn't a fixed destination but a continual learning process. It's about evolving your habits, adapting to new information, and constantly recognizing the more profound ethical implications of your clothes. As you deepen your understanding of this field, you'll find yourself naturally embodying the key Buddhist principles of mindfulness, simplicity, and compassion – not just in your attire, but as a living, breathing part of your everyday existence.

As you wear your clothes, remember you're not just adorning your body, but also practicing a lifestyle more attuned to the interconnectedness of the universe, reflecting a commitment to conscientious living and compassion for all beings. This guide is but a stepping stone into this wider world, and we hope it illuminates your sartorial path with wisdom and compassion.

Let us call to heart the Buddha's words in our quest for enlightened fashion: "We are what we think, all that we are arises with our thoughts, with our thoughts we make the world." Let's make the world better, one conscious fashion choice at a time.

Chapter 7. Compassionate Fashion: Empathising with Craftsmanship

As we begin our exploration into compassionate fashion, let us first dive deep into the realm of craftsmanship. Craftsmanship represents the heart and soul of any piece of clothing; it encapsulates the dedication, commitment, and expertise of a person or a group of people who laboriously invest their time, effort, and skills into creating a product.

7.1. Appreciating the Art of Craftsmanship

Just as the Buddha emphasizes the importance of understanding the impermanence and interconnectedness of all things, appreciating the artistry in craftsmanship requires a similar level of cognizance. With each stitch, tie, cut, and embellishment, a unique story is woven into the garment. A story that speaks of the meticulous efforts of the craftsperson, the beautiful journey the raw materials have undergone, and the environmental impact of the production process.

To empathize with craftsmanship is to fully understand and appreciate all the elements involved in the creation of your wardrobe. It's about valuing the time, skill, and dedication that a craftsperson has invested in fashioning a piece of clothing. Empathy towards craftsmanship also entails a deep respect for the resources that have been used—and those that have been preserved—in the production process. In essence, it invites a kindness towards all the lives touched by each garment, from the creator to the wearer.

7.2. The Skilled Hands Behind the Seams

Consider, for a moment, your favorite article of clothing. Reflect on the textures, the unique details, and the comfort it brings you. Now, imagine the individuals who lent their skills to your clothing piece—their time, their labour, their dedication. The fabric weaver who deftly maneuvered threads into beautiful patterns. The dye artist who breathed life into the yarn with vibrant hues. The cutter who shaped the material, the seamstress who skillfully sewed the seams, the finisher who added the final touches. Each step involved an artisan, a master of their craft.

By acknowledging their work and understanding the concentration and precision each process demands, we not only foster a deeper connection with our clothing but also cultivate an immense respect for the individuals and methods behind them.

7.3. Making Mindful Purchases

Buddhism places great emphasis on mindfulness, and it's a principle that applies equally to our fashion choices. When purchases are made mindfully—when consideration is given to how a piece is made, who has made it, and its environmental impact—we not only signal respect for craftsmanship but become a part of a compassionate supply chain. Look for brands that aren't just stylish, but also ethical and sustainable. They should be transparent about their production processes, and ensure that their craftsmen are paid fairly, and work in safe environments.

7.4. The Beauty of Handmade Artistry

In the world of fast fashion, the essence of traditional artistry often goes unnoticed. Handcrafted garments carry within them intricacies that are missing in the mass-produced items. The irregular stitches, the slight variance in color shades, the inconsistent patterns—these are the marks of human hands, a testament to individuality and authenticity. By valuing and preferring this uniqueness over machine-made uniformity, you are empathizing with the hard work, creativity, and spirit of the artisan.

7.5. Cherishing Craftsmanship

Finally, it's about cherishing what you own. True appreciation for craftsmanship can be demonstrated by how you respect and care for your garments. Extend their life by washing at the right temperatures, air drying instead of tumble drying, repairing instead of replacing. These steps are simple, but they ensure the hard work of the artisans does not go to waste.

The journey towards compassionate fashion is not merely about style transformation—it encourages us to embrace the beauty of slow, mindful living. It asks us to take a moment, savor the details, acknowledge the effort, and express gratitude for everything that makes our style uniquely ours. By practicing empathy towards craftsmanship, we not only make personal fashion statements but become torchbearers of a compassionate, sustainable fashion movement.

Chapter 8. Impermanence and Adaptability in Fashion Trends

To truly grasp the concepts of impermanence and adaptability in fashion trends, we must first delve into the Buddhist principle of Anicca, or the doctrine of impermanence. From this viewpoint, we can begin to explore the seamless transience of fashion trends and how they are intrinsically linked to our intrinsic human nature of change and evolution.

8.1. The Principle of Anicca: A Buddhist Perspective

The Buddhist doctrine of Anicca posits that all of existence, all phenomena, are subject to change and are therefore transient. In the context of fashion, this principle can be seen as a reflection on the transient nature of trends. The evolution of fashion seasons, the constant introduction of fresh designs, the fading of trends only to be resurfaced — all beautifully encapsulate the teachings of Anicca.

In the conventional world, the cyclicality of trends can often drive a form of consumption that contradicts with the principles of sustainability and mindful living. However, diving deeper into the realm of Anicca, we can embrace this transience as a challenge to adapt and evolve with compassion for the environment and respect for ancient wisdom.

8.2. Transience of Fashion Trends: A Mirror to Anicca

Fashion, in many ways, exemplifies the Buddhist concept of impermanence. Everything about fashion – the way trends emerge, peak, fade, and then are reincarnated – mirrors the ebbs and flows of life itself.

Just as the only constant in life is change, the only certain thing in fashion is the cyclical nature of trends. The power of this parallel lies in how they unravel a deeper layer of understanding when approached mindfully.

Yet, while the Buddhist philosophy of Anicca urges us to accept impermanence as inherent to existence, it doesn't advocate for constant desire or indulgence. Instead, it asks us to adapt to change with keen awareness and morality, also a crucial lesson for style enthusiasts.

8.3. Adaptability: The Antidote to Impermanence

Fashion is a vibrant industry that thrives on versatility, creativity, and constant evolution. As trends begin to wane, new ones take root, rendering what was 'in' yesterday out of vogue today. This consistent shift may seem like a threat to a sustainable lifestyle. However, when viewed through the Buddhist lens, these shifts can actually serve as an opportunity to employ adaptability – the antidote to impermanence.

Adapting to trend changes doesn't mean compulsively shopping each season. It means evolving our wardrobe in a mindful manner, considering economic, social, and environmental factors. True adaptability in fashion comes from celebrating individual style over fast trends. By focusing on timeless pieces, incorporating sustainable practices, and personalizing your style, you can embrace change while espousing the Buddhist values of compassion and mindfulness.

8.4. Application of Anicca and Adaptability in Styling

Wondering how to apply the concepts of Anicca and adaptability to your personal style?

The answer is remarkably simple: focus on mindful consumption and value quality over quantity. Choose versatile pieces that can be styled in various ways and transcend the bounds of seasons. Incorporate clothing that can adapt to different style narratives and encourage a minimalistic and sustainable approach in building your wardrobe.

By practicing these principles, men can take fashion trends in stride with the changing tides, allowing for a seamless blend of conscious style and Buddhist principles.

8.5. Fashion as Acts of Kindness: A Tranquil Marriage of Style and Compassion

Drawing parallels between the Buddhist teachings and fashion isn't about creating a showy display of stylish garments. Instead, it's about cultivating an understanding that even mundane actions, like dressing, can be acts of loving-kindness.

Such acts can be as simple as choosing ethically sourced clothing, minimizing waste by opting for recyclable or biodegradable materials, or even expressing empathy through clothing choices that embrace inclusive sizing or companies that support the underprivileged.

In the end, the understanding of impermanence in fashion trends urges us to conceive our wardrobe thoughtfully, nurturing an adaptable style that reflects our inner tranquility and compassion. It opens avenues to explore fashion as not just a means to look good but to feel good and do good to oneself and the world.

8.6. Embracing Anicca and Adaptability: A Path Towards Enlightened Fashion

As we journey through the unpredictable world of fashion, the Buddhist teachings of Anicca and the trait of adaptability can guide us towards a more conscious and compassionate involvement with style. These principles can inspire us to break free from the shackles of fast fashion, helping us to cultivate a mindful and versatile wardrobe.

Remember, the goal isn't to shun trends or disregard fashion. Instead, it's about understanding fashion's transient nature and using it as a medium for personal and communal growth. By embracing change, flexibly adapting to trends with mindfulness, and nurturing our unique style, we can courageously embark on a journey of enlightened fashion.

By inception to end, this chapter reflects the Buddhist teachings of Anicca, mindfulness, and the importance of adaptability. It's a path that enables us to explore the intricate relationship between fashion and spirituality, urging us to transform fashion choices into acts of compassion, thus bringing our clothing in alignment with our spiritual values.

Chapter 9. Dress Well, Do Good: Ethical Consumerism in Men's Style

Folks say that clothes make the man. Thousands of years of wisdom from Buddhist teachings tell us it isn't just about the clothes we don but about the intentions and actions making those clothes possible. So, shopping isn't merely a matter of style but also of mindfulness and ethics. This is where ethical consumerism weds men's fashion.

9.1. Understanding Ethical Consumerism

Ethical consumerism is the practice of selecting products and services produced in a way that minimizes social and environmental harm, while maximizing positive impact. This includes everything from the clothes you wear to the coffee you drink.

Buddhist teachings emphasize on 'right livelihood,' which is about making a living in a way that doesn't cause harm or suffering. One could extend this philosophy to our consumption practices too. When we choose ethically produced clothing, we are indirectly promoting a 'right livelihood' for those involved in the production. We're supporting companies that treat their workers fairly and responsibly manage their environmental impact.

9.2. The Significance of Ethical Brands

Ethics should be more than a mere consideration in fashion; they become an imperative part of the wardrobe. As consumers, we have a powerful tool at our disposal to effect change in the fashion industry: our purchasing power. When that power is coupled with mindful reflection upon the conditions under which our clothing was produced, it engages a powerful lever of change.

Every dollar spent is a vote cast for the kind of world we want. Ethical brands take steps to ensure their products are made with respect for people and the planet. They prioritize fair wages and safe working conditions. They minimize their environmental impact through strategies like using eco-friendly materials and implementing waste reduction measures. Supporting these brands is a means of translating the principles of compassion and right livelihood into action.

9.3. Spotting The Ethically Made

Of course, merely wanting to support ethical brands isn't enough. We need to identify them. Transparency, fairness, sustainability, and compassion are key traits of ethically made clothing. Does the brand disclose its supply chain and labor practices? Does it ensure fair wages and safe working conditions? Does it seek to minimize its environmental footprint? Does it show compassion not only to human life but also to animals by eschewing materials resulting from animal cruelty?

Looking for certifications can help. Certifications like Fair Trade, Global Organic Textile Standard (GOTS), and Certified B Corporations are strong indicators of ethical production practices.

9.4. Dapper and Compassionate: Ethical Style Inspiration

Fortunately, ethical fashion doesn't mean sacrificing style. Brands like Patagonia, People Tree, and Nudie Jeans are testament to the fact that one can be fashion-forward and environmentally conscious simultaneously.

Patagonia is renowned for its sustainable outdoor clothing and its commitment to the environment. Similarly, People Tree, one of the pioneers in ethical and sustainable fashion, designs stylish apparel made from 100% organic cotton and other sustainable materials, while ensuring fair trade practices. Nudie Jeans emphasizes the longevity of products, offering repair services to extend the life of their denim.

Finding a balance between being stylish and being mindful can create a harmonious relationship with yourself and the world around you.

9.5. Your Clothing, Your Practice

Buddha said, "Every morning we are born again. What we do today matters most." Your fashion choices can be an embodiment of this teaching. Each time you decide to purchase a piece of clothing, remind yourself that this decision isn't just about you, but about the larger world you are a part of.

Your attire can be a significant part of your mindfulness practice. Each time you don an ethically-produced shirt or pair of trousers, it's a reminder of your commitment to do good, be compassionate, and live consciously. To walk the path of Buddhist teachings isn't just about meditation on a cushion; it's about how we navigate every aspect of our lives, including the seemingly mundane act of purchasing clothes.

By choosing with intention, we can sow seeds of goodness with every garment. Mindful wardrobe choices can be a complement to our daily practices of awareness, compassion, moderation, and wisdom.

Chapter 10. Inner Peace meets Outer Style: Representing Your Inner Zen

The recognition of one's real nature, an unveiling of their inward spirit through outward projection, is the meeting point of inner peace and outer style. The journey begins with exploring a mindfulness-based approach towards fashion, where your clothing is not merely a physical entity but an embodiment of your internal essence.

10.1. Mindfulness and Style

Mindfulness is a crucial Buddhist principle that encourages living in the present moment, acknowledging your thoughts and feelings without judgement. This seemingly simple concept has profound implications when applied to your style. Mindfulness involves stepping away from the fast-paced, trend-driven fashion world, and focusing on personal style that echoes your sensibilities and inner peace.

Identifying and understanding the emotions affiliated with your clothes is the first step towards mindful wardrobe cultivation. Recall this: When you last wore that jacket, did it make you feel confident? Does the color of your shirt affect your mood? Exploring these questions can provide significant insights into what truly suits you, not just physically, but emotionally.

10.2. The Tranquil Language of Colors

Color plays a significant role in Buddhist symbolism, each color representing different aspects of Buddha's teachings. Similarly, the colors you wear significantly influence your emotions, and, by extension, your style. In fact, studies reveal that colors can inspire emotions ranging from tranquility to excitement. For example, while blue is associated with calm and peace, red conveys passion, and yellow, joy.

A tranquil wardrobe predominantly features colors that promote calmness and positivity, in essence, reflecting your inner Zen. Begin by familiarizing yourself with the meanings attached to each color, subsequently selecting those that resonate with your sense of tranquility.

10.3. The Serene Appeal of Minimalism

Buddhism promotes simplicity, a life free from unnecessary clutter. A minimalist approach to style embraces this idea, focusing on necessities and quality rather than excess. It suggests investing in well-made, timeless pieces instead of hopping on every fashion trend. Minimalism does not mean a lacklustre wardrobe; on the contrary, it celebrates the power of simplicity.

An overloaded wardrobe can be stressful; a minimalist wardrobe, on the other hand, reduces this noise. Each piece in your collection should serve a purpose, be it functional like protecting you from the weather, or emotional, like making you feel joyful. This idea supports the tenet of right consumption in Buddhism, which not only emphasizes judicious buying but also environmental consciousness.

10.4. Patterned Peace: Symbolism in Designs

The rich tapestry of Buddhist art is replete with symbolic patterns. Spirals stand for the path to enlightenment, lotuses represent purity, while the endless knot symbolizes interconnectedness. Such deeply embedded symbolism can translate to clothing, too. For instance, incorporating lotus patterns can serve as a reminder for purity of thought, or wearing a spiral design could represent your journey towards self-discovery and peace.

10.5. Crafting Compassionate Choices

At the heart of Buddhism lies compassion, for oneself and others. An enlightened sartorial approach should not only hinge on personal contentment but also considerate choices. This includes being mindful of where and how your clothes are made, thereby promoting ethical and sustainable fashion. Embracing organic fabrics, shunning animal-sourced materials, and supporting fair-trade and worker-friendly brands align with the Buddhist principle of 'right livelihood.'

10.6. Protection of Peace: Caring for Your Clothing

An important aspect of transforming your style to reflect your inner Zen is caring for your clothes. This goes beyond routine maintenance. From washing to storing and mending, every care ritual bears a meditative quality. Mending a torn pocket or sewing a button, for example, is not just about fixing clothes; it's about appreciating their value and prolonging their lifespan. Such acts subtly echo the concept of impermanence, reminding us of the transient nature of material things.

10.7. Ultimately, You

Your journey to style enlightenment is uniquely yours. You do not need to suddenly mutate your wardrobe to follow these tenets. Real change, as Buddhism acknowledges, is gradual, stemming from consistent mindfulness. So start by understanding these principles and applying them in small, manageable ways to your style. Allow your inner Zen to slowly surface and inform your sartorial choices, resulting in a wardrobe that not only pleases the eye, but also the mind, ultimately a distinctive manifestation of who you truly are.

Stepping into the world of style with a fresh perspective empowered by mindfulness, an understanding of symbolic colors and designs, a commitment to care, and compassion could be just the beginning. This journey won't just change the way you dress, but it will change you. Because, after all, what is style but an understated narrative of evolution and identity? At the end of this voyage, you will see how 'fashion with compassion' can be a path towards the dharma of dressing, reflecting your true self and embracing inner peace.

Through "The Buddha's Guide to Men's Style: Fashion with Compassion", it is hoped that the wholesome vision of personal style transcends the confines of your wardrobe and seeps into other aspects of life as well. May you dress with dignity and depth, courage and compassion, wisdom and warmth, mindful of the threads that connect us all.

Chapter 11. Conclusion: Harnessing the Power of Compassionate Fashion

In the enthralling journey we've traversed together through "The Buddha's Guide to Men's Style: Fashion with Compassion," we've laid down the stepping stones in synchronizing style and Buddhist approach. This journey was not merely about choosing the right tie or trouser but transcending the superficial levels of fashion to a spiritual plain — utilizing our choices to cultivate mindfulness, wisdom, and compassion. We now exist in the eye-opening semisphere where our image is not just about visual glitz but reverberates our consciousness and empathy.

11.1. The Interplay of Fashion and Mindfulness

Mindfulness is the heart of Buddhism, encouraging an awake and present mentality. An integral element of this philosophy asks us to be conscious and deliberate in our daily actions, and this extends to our fashion choices. Mundane activities, like putting on clothes, can be transformed into opportunities for deliberate mindfulness when taken into the Buddhist perspective.

Our fashion decisions are no longer impulsive buys or driven by fleeting trends; instead, they've evolved into insightful selections that mirror not just who we are but how we perceive the world and our place within it. Wearing an outfit becomes a ritualistic act of mindfulness, each piece of clothing, an embodiment of our commitment to this path. Each step taken to preserve the clothes, respecting the hands that had crafted them, echoing gratitude and understanding towards the interconnectedness in our world.

11.2. Style as a Means of Cultivating Compassion

Central to the Buddhist ethos is compassion, a realization of shared human experience and a commitment to alleviate collective suffering. When we understand our clothing, not as mere objects but as conduits of our intentions — we start harnessing the power of compassionate fashion.

Let us revisit the parable of the monk's robe, a reminder of humble and ethical self-expression, which imparts wisdom and serves as a beacon of compassion. Today, our fashion choices can be a direct extension of this compassion, emphasizing ethical production, sustainable sourcing, and fair trade. By making these conscious sartorial decisions, we contribute towards ameliorating suffering for both the planet and its inhabitants.

11.3. Sartorial Wisdom in Your Everyday

The Buddha urges us to find wisdom in the everyday moment — an insight that applies splendidly to our wardrobe. Each time we look into our closets, we can see reflections of our journey towards mindful fashion, affirming the gentle balance between appearance and essence.

Combining an effortless style that resonates our personality with clothes that aesthetically align with our inner values opens an invigorating avenue, a meaningful way to express our sartorial wisdom. Empathy and humility echo in the choice of a simple shirt crafted with sustainable methods, as they do in a well-tailored suit that fits not just your form but your ethos too.

11.4. Fashion as a Tool for Positive Changes

By fully integrating mindful fashion, we become instrumental in creating positive changes. The ripple effect of our fashion choices can influence not just ourselves but those around us, and eventually, the entire fashion industry. It's an ever-expanding, self-perpetuating cycle of affirmative fashion changes where the consumer and supplier influence and evolve with each other.

The importance of this holistic approach to men's fashion can never be overstated. It is not just an upgrade to your personal style; it's a step towards a greater vision — a world where everyone recognizes the impact of their clothing choices, and works in harmony with each other and the environment.

11.5. Embracing the Path of Compassionate Fashion

From mindful selections of apparel to sustaining the life of our clothing through conscious care, we've progressively harnessed the power of compassionate fashion. As we've learned, fashion viewed through a Buddhist lens is not just about looking good; it's about feeling good and doing good.

May this knowledge serve you well as you walk this path. Remember that this sartorial journey, as with all aspects of life, is ever-evolving. We each have the potential to learn, grow, and contribute positively to the world through our fashion. Let your style not just make you stand out in a crowd, but reflect the compassion, wisdom, and humility chiseled within you.

Indeed, this isn't a conclusion, but another starting point in your journey of compassionate fashion. As you step out in your mindfully selected apparel, embodying kindness and understanding, let your every stride reverberate the tranquil yet powerful teachings of the Buddha. Garner the positive energy that compassionate fashion brings along — continue to cultivate mindfulness, and evolve – on the inside, on the outside, in wardrobe selections, in life.

Seeing beyond trends and fads, learning that fashion is more than mere aesthetics and superficiality, we, together, have harnessed the power of compassionate fashion. Your fashion is your statement. Let it echo the Buddhist principles of compassion, wisdom, and humility. Make it strong, make it resonant. After all, style is not just what you wear; it is who you are.

www.ingramcontent.com/pod-product-compliance
Lightning Source LLC
Chambersburg PA
CBHW072220290526
45794CB00007B/2816